Train of 'unthoughts'

AF632827

Lauren Higgins

BookLeaf Publishing

Presentation by *BookLeaf Publishing*

Web: www.bookleafpub.com

E-mail: info@bookleafpub.com

ISBN: 9789395950121

First edition 2022

DEDICATION

This book is dedicated to Gran Nan A.K.A 'Monkey Nan' (Gladys Hill) and 'Poppy Dennis' (Dennis Hill) . The true poets of the family - Thankyou for passing on your gift and guiding me along the way.

ACKNOWLEDGEMENT

Thankyou to everyone who believed in and encouraged me along the way, but a very special thankyou to my lovely friend - Bethannie Jackson.

PREFACE

Social media is always in my face- The times are screens; and the worlds so invested.
I needed a break, I was asking for a sign..

An Ad on Facebook kept popping up . About writting a poetry book - A 21 day challenge- I'd ignore it multiple times until I had a thought..
I said to myself, if I see this ad again I'll take it as a sign..if I dont- I won't go looking for it..
I opened the app, and you know what was there?..first thing!..right in my face!.. was the ad to write a poetry book!!

So here I am with all my 'unthoughts' - guided poems from my passed loved ones.

'A crimson tide'

A crimson Tide begins to rise, the sunset hides
behind the skies.
To a place of unknowing it's set to go, the place
where you are? I don't know.

It reaches the crest and darkness fades, the
sunset now, dark grey shades.
Just like my heart, when I seen you die; a sunset
fading with a darkened sky.

The crest is dark now, the sun has gone.
Blackness falls on the valley that once shone.
Just like your presence when you disappeared;
shades of darkness crept in near.

I stayed in that darkness for some time, I battled
to see, I struggled to climb. I could feel the
strength of the crimson Tide but I waited still for
that valley to shine..

I waited and I watched- the blackness and tide.
No longer crimson but dark inside, I couldn't
deal- with the dark surrounds; my heart was
sinking, I felt I had drowned..

I thought I should give up, and float out to sea, float with the tide; with the sunset and be free..

But I raised my head, then only to see, the shine of the moon casting light over me.
It was enough light; to see my way, enough of a hope that I'll Concur this grey.

I swam back to shore, i followed that moon, I climbed that crest, and soon then I knew; I knew I felt close, closer to the top, I realised, that's now the past; and that I never lost.

I turned my back from where that sunset, knowing that way was to darkness and a drowning death, once I faced the other way, I seen a sunrise forming a light of day.

That once crimson Tide had sunken back, the way it looked was no longer black, it had a shine to it, a clearer sight; a new casting shine from a new days light.

A blue, a white and a deep warm feel. But the horrowing journey in darkness was a greater ordeal...would it swollen me again, would I learn how to swim? Can I face the darkness, and find the light once again?

A new day starts but it will always end, this time
I'll watch the sunset with my family or a friend.

'Fork in the road'

There's a fork in the road-

Is it going to lead to a path of the unknown?

A New fork in the road-

Oh which one of you will take me home?

If I choose a path-
That I can not see-
How will I know my destiny?

There's a fork in the road-

Give me a sign to lead me home.

If I follow the path that my heart feels-
Will it lead me home? Or will I take on a thrill?

So I close my eyes
Imagine a place of beauty
I place myself in a world of peace,
I escape my hurt and inner scrutiny.

There's fields of flowers

Blooming in shades of dashing gold;
The breeze sleeks on by my ears, like a kiss
from a heavens hold.

Follow your heart, you've got stories to be told-

Open your eyes-

Now where's that fork in the road?

'Missing you...'

Sometimes you just come to me,
Your presence reappears.
I never know why it is,
I haven't seen you- in many years!

I hear you in my thoughts,
I feel you standing near.
I never can be too sure of it,
But I just know when you are here!

After a while I check the date,
your prepping me now, I know,
This dreaded time comes around again,
The time we had to let you go!

It's a different type of missing you,
When this time comes every year.
It's a replay of the grief we feel,
The pain of indescribable fear!

I always think of what you said to me,
Before you left us here on earth.
I hope your playing that guitar Pop!!
I hope Heaven knows your worth!! 🖤

'Pearls' - by 'Monkey Nan'

Pearls

Life gave to me - a necklace so rare
Of perfect small pearls - linked with love and with care
Each representing - the ones I hold dear
Some I have lost - are no longer here
On my necklace of life - we aren't really apart
For they're worn by me always - close to my heart
Centre pearl of my gift - my partner in life
Who so long ago - chose me for his wife
Then others were added - a daughter and sons
Tied closely together - with their special ones
Over the years come more precious pearls
In the shape of small boys - petite little girls
Sisters and brother - much loved part of my piece
Favourite cousins and aunts, nephews and niece
Special old friends are threaded there too
So much a part of the things that I do
I am so thankful - as time slowly unfurls
To be linked on through life - with my precious pearls

For love cannot be bought - it's beautiful and
free
Yet my treasured necklace is priceless to me

Gladys Hill

'Grief and acceptance'

I hate that you were right in telling me, that you
wernt coming home..
You knew It, and had accepted it, but still told
me all alone..
You prepared me for the moment, by being blunt
with oh such care...
You said "Wally I'm not coming home from
theatre- I'm going to play for the big guy up
there"...
I laughed and told you not to be silly, your
coming home to play for me...
You said "No Wall I'm not, My Mum come and
visit me"
I knew you were right- but apart of me didn't
want to agree, so I laughed again and fobbed
you off again- said "see you in a couple weeks"
💔

4 years now since you've been gone and not a
day goes by that I don't replay that conversation
and wish I took you more serious..

I know the guitar pick that I placed in your
hands, has been helpful for playing Copperhead
road for the big guy 🎸

Miss you old man 👴

'Dust'

Pockets of dust,
How can I over come,
Emptiness, shadows;
Heart beating loud like a drum.

Racing yet watching;
Sitting silently and still.
Filling my pockets full of sand,
As I sit alone on the dusty hill.

Winds whistling, a breeze,
Drifts on over, oh so near.
My eyes are full of sand now,
The dust, makes it blurry, unclear.

Raking rocks against my eyeballs,
The dust seems so hard to clear.
The harder I try to clean my eyes,
The deeper the pain in them appears.

Wasting time- Stop rubbing them.
The dust is actually sand.
Take a moment - Gather yourself.
Reach outwards with your hands.

Remove the grains with patience,
Water, and your friends.
The pain in them will disappear
The hurt- it will mend.

Help is near- It's never far away;
You were never alone on that hill.
You just sat by yourself you see,
And the dust began to fill-

You pockets,-
Your eyes, your heart and head.
The grains became so deep you see,
Cutting you - thread, by thread.

You were burdened
But by your own sandy feet.
Getting cut by grains of sand.
This feeling was on repeat

In your wounds- it hurt, the pain
Until you reached out,
Because you just thought it was dust
There was no need to shout.

Reach out while it's in your pockets
Don't let dust turn into sand.

Don't rub it in your wounds.
Dust it off and make a stand !

'Not a poet'

I sat and wrote-
These words one day,
I just started writting-
I didn't know what to say.

These words as I write them-
They begin to flow.
I'm not sure what it is-
I just let the pen go.

It glides across the paper-
Like i know what to write,
But I havnt a clue really-
In actual hindsight;

Like this sentence right now-
They're just words to me,
But somehow I join them-
To make a word symphony.

Could I be a poet?-
But I just write down words;
They rhyme and flow though,
Sounding like a songs verse.

I really don't mean to do it-
It's like my brain has its own tongue.
I do find it satisfying,
Interesting and fun.

Now I havnt a clue-
What I'm about to write,
The words start flowing-
The pen takes flight.

Some times I can't keep up-
The melodies flowing from my head.
The pen gets faster writting,
It's like an ink spill that's sped-

In a writting hurry;
The papers covered in ink.
These words though I've written,
I didn't even have to think..

Am I a poet?
Who has a skill for this text?
Passed down from one generation-
To the other and the next..?

'Your a plant'

Your alive,

You breathe,

You feel,

You bleed.

Your a plant in disguise-

Blossom,

Grow,

And Thrive.

Get some sunlight,

Bathe in the rain,

Stay hydrated,

Rest in the shade.

Take care little plant-

Let your leaves grow!

Thrive in your own time-

Your destined to glow!

'Nature's child'

Shes a bare foot beauty,
Hears the birds chirp and tweet.
Follows the sounds,
Of rivers and creeks.

The dirt will wash off,
Her hair combed and clean.
Her sun kissed skin,
The grass stains her knees green.

She has splinters in her hands,
And a graze on her knee.
Yet she does not care,
She likes being free.

It's the simple things in life-
The things people take for granted.
Yet you have always treasured them,
And been one to share them.

-Sleeps under the stars,
Lets rivers sweep through her feet.
Wind blows in her hair,
Wild flowers- smell sweet.

Adventure and nature,
It's her place to be.
In her element of belonging,
Yet her way to feel free!

For my nature loving girl- Allayah

'Tamworth bound'

It was a long drive down-
2 and a bit hours.
It felt like forever,
Pops car hadn't much power.
We would go all the back roads,
Call into the small towns and see-
The local takeaway ladies,
Get a feed- do a wee.
Back on the road -
We would finally go,
After pop lit his Durrie,
And wound down his window.
Tamworth outskirts-
Were finally nearer than afar.
I was surprised we got there-
In pops old Celica.
We would pull up in the drive way,
Of Lemon Gums Drive.
After a long day of travel -
2 and a bit, turned to 5.
Gran Nan would be waiting,
At the top of the stairs,
Come running down, arms open,
High and kisses to spare.
"Come in, come in" ,

She would say with a smile,
"I'll put the kettle on,
"Dinner will be ready In a while".

"I've put on a roast" -
And I could tell by the smell.
Nans Roast lamb and veggies
Will go down quite well.
We would take in our bags,
And settle inside.
Then pop would have a cuppa,
After his long drive.
Nan had the old kitchen,
with fuzzy carpet on the floor.
She had mirrors above the stairs,
That would cover the whole wall.
Down stairs she had a room,
That looked like pub or bar.
And her garage was well big enough,
To fit at least 4 cars.
Her yard was filled with lovely-
Shrubs and blooming flowers.
She would be out there gardening,
For quite a few hours.
"Dinners nearly ready" -
She would yell out loud.
" Go wash your hands with soap!"
"And Dry them on the towel"
"Your plates are in the oven"

"Be careful now they're hot"
"I'll dish up your dinner"
"go sit and choose your spot"

After dinner was done
We would wash the dishes with Nan
"Wash the dishes, dry the dishes"
She so happily Sang
Soon it would be time
To climb up into bed,
"Good night Gran Nan, Love you"
and she would kiss me on the head.

'Memories of 'Den-ass'

The strings would move,
The pick would bounce,
The sound of music,
Comes echoing out.

The leg crossed over,
The feet tap to the beat,
The rhythm he would make-
The atmosphere a treat.

The black filtered butt-
On his rolled cigarette,
Would hang from his mouth,
as he sang copperhead.

He would look up to watch,
His grandkids dancing about.
Whilst nan's in the kitchen,
Singing the songs loud.

His crosswords there,
Beside him to do.
It's the little memories 'Den-ass',
That we treasure of you.

Drives in the celica,
Cheeky jokes that you'd play.
Your paintings, green tree frogs,
Cricket, chocolate frappes.

You taught us all-
some great values in life.
Like stick out your tongue,
Eat extra sweets at night.

So now that we're here,
We've laid you down to rest.
We'll all treasure your memories,
And know we were blessed.

For your book may have closed,
Before your chapter could end.
But we will keep your story going,
And share the memories we've spent.

(Written and read for Pops funeral service)

'Face of clouds'

When the sun sets,
I look to the sky.
I wonder what your doing,
Way up there high.
I imagine you watching us,
Looking down on us 3.
Playing your guitar,
Smiling, happy and free.
We form your face in the clouds,
It helps the way we see.
You looking down over us,
Over your grandchildren and me.
We talk of you often,
Think of you every day.
The girls ask me questions,
So we visit you and play.
We sitting apon your grave site,
Wishing you were still here.
Then we leave you once again,
with a painful heart and a tear.
But we know your watching us,
Although we can not see you.
So we imagine your face in the clouds,
Your face of clouds we drew.

'The feral family'

Dennis- a tall slender man,
with dark curly hair,
Met a pretty young woman,
who's skin wasnt fair.
They lived in Yallaroi -
off an old dirt track-
Somewhere past Warialda,
I can't be exact.
They set up their life -
were quickly married infact.
They then had a child -
there was no doubt about that.
They named her Tracie,
Tracie Lee to be precise,
And wasn't she sweet,
oh so ever nice.

They then went on to have -
another child you see.
Another little girl - named Talia Maree.
She had the same hair
just like her sister before.
But something was different,
she was quite a handful more.

Now off Dennis goes-
to work on the rails.
Leaving his pretty wife,
to raise his ferals.
But more children they add,
Another girl - what a joy.
A little girl with blonde curls,
named coreena- But still no boy.
And off Dennis would go again,
to work and to see-
His mates he played in a band with-
All probably piss pots if you ask me.
But alas Dennis would return home,
With his earnings and his pride
For he was a hard working man
And a pretty woman was his bride.

They opted again,
Well atleast i think they did,
Along come Mark Douglas-
A striking young kid.
Eventually Cheryl the bride said
"this is it, I've had enough,
I can't raise kids on a farm,
It's awfully fecking tough"
So they packed all their belongings
And hopped in the car.
Arriving at Inverell, it wasn't too far.
They found a little house,

in a - Medora street.
They unpacked the car, set up camp-
without the sheep.
Put the kids in school,
watched them grow.
Suddenly they're all adults,
with feral of their own.

The Medora house has had so many-
Fingerprints plastered on its walls.
Not only from those ferals -
but the next lot that was born.
Life can be unpredictable-
have it's ups and downs.
But simple little memories -
Keep my feral family around.

'From Son to Mum' - By Dennis Hill

My dearest 'GLADARSE' !!

The deepest of love and trust, of hope and fears. We've both shared together for seventy years. When I was a child- I depended on you. To nurture and care, amd get me through. To teach me life's values, to mould my young mind.Honesty, Hard work, and the gift to be kind. We were on the same wave length, spirits soared free, and shared a heavenly gift of telepathy.
Caring and sharing- the ordeals of life 'til I was a man and brougt home a young wife. You loved and accepted her just as your own. And over the years the kids came along. Four grandchildren, three girls and a boy, gave you hours of hard work, pleasure and joy. And as I look back - over the years. Theres been lots of laughter, not many tears. Now your peacefully resting with your precious few. I'm honoured and privileged, to be part of you..

With all our everlasting love -

"DENARSE", Cheryl and the tribe xxxx

'Lost - burnt out Mother'

My patience has gone.

I can't savour any more.

I can't hold in my anger,

my frustrations- my core-

my inner demon that fires inside,

it kills me now....my patience has died.

I use to be able to smile and not care,

now I boil and explode-

I pull out my hair.

I'm not sure if this is what you call weak?

or is this an expression of exhaustion-

because I'm at my peak!?

'To my girls' - Allayah, Sophie and Claire

When you were born,
I seen my life;
A love forever-
That will always suffice.
You are my heart
My world, my dream.
There is no one -
That could come between.
My sweet, my love, my baby for life;
May you always see my smile -
Not my sacrifice.
My pride, my joy, my miracle babe;
You knew how to shape mumma-
In a positive way.
My soul, my breathe, my little mini me;
Please always stay close my dear-
Close beside me.
Don't stray too far now
My dear child of mine.
For your forever my babies
My heart and soul undefined.
My world wouldn't be,
As I know it right now;
If you grew up too fast

And didn't need mumma - how!?
Stay young my girls-
Be a sweet child at heart;
Your mumma dosnt want you to grow up too fast
🩶

'AUGUST'

Magpies land on the washing line.

Dandelions Blossoming with their golden shine.

Crisp autumn leaves have almost gone.

The Sunshines warmer, the days get long.

The wood piles empty, The grass grows green.

The season of spring, its felt before seen.

Neighbours mowing their lawn, Kids playing outside.

You hear them kicking ball, til 8pm some nights.

Salads with dinner, the camp chairs come out.

Mozzies start bitting, Flies are buzzing about.

The feeling of spring is already here -
The calender just says otherwise this year.

'Frog lies'

Little green frog- why do you tell lies.
Croaking 'bout rain- when we've got blue skies.
If you will persist- and we don't get soaked.
Your "end" will come swiftly- (captured and
choked).
It's very frustrating- when you croak all the day.
Just because water in the drains rush away.

By Glady Hill

'Change your perspective'

If we could change lives-then just MAYBE.
We may be nicer to each other you see..

Perspective dosnt happens when one puts aside -
not acknowledging the struggles ones had in
their lives.

Judgement takes over from one's first impression
or view- we never actually ask "Hey, what made
you, YOU "

If we could swap lives- maybe we'd see,
If I could be you- and you could be me.

If we could change worlds- then we would
know,
What it took for each other to grow.

I'd know your struggles and you would know
mine,
We could help each other after- see more eye to
eye.

SO it's not about your place or where you stow,
It's about the struggles it took for you to grow!

'Train of unthoughts'

The tracks facing north,
Headn' to the valley where the sunshines,
Crisply in the morning,
melting frost from clothes lines.

The trains from the coal era,
It dosnt run on electricity,
Load it up with power,
From chunks of coal you see.

Fires blazing up,
steams in the whistles hold.
Ready to take on adventures,
Great stories to be told.

Sit on comfy in your seat,
Near a window with a view.
Now watch on as the train sets off,
Taking its thoughts from you.

You loose your mind in yellow fields,
Of canola and sunflower seed.
You start thinking of the golden glow,
How the sun shines, the birds fly free.

You watch the rivers run along,
Beside the train and its track.
And see the rains its brought on down,
From the valleys - within its cracks.

Farms and fields of horses -
Local honey with buzzing bees,
Sheep manure for sale,
Set under the shade of trees.

A store and the farm land-
In that quick small glimpse,
From the window of the train,
You can get so many hints.

Of the life and people around you-
As they flash and zoom on by,
Giving you a train of thought -
Unthought though in your mind.

'Old summer days'

Bare foot walking in the summers sun,
Worry less- free, searching for fun.
Building a Billy cart, jumping on hay-
Oh what I'd do now for THOSE summer days!

Riding the bikes as far as we could go,
Getting to the hills that made us go slow,
Turning around to roll all the way -
Back home for some more mischief and play.

Big ropes we would pull- up to the trees
Attach tyre, make swings, fall, scrape our knees.
cubby houses and tents, fields to explore.
The Imagination we had- ideas galore!

The neighbouring kids would all come out, we
would make up more games -
Adventures and scout
The local bushland, the graveyard and hills
Exploring the area, fulfilling our thrills.

Pushing some limits
without any care
Living the free life-
As kids do - unaware.

Riding home barefoot on a summers night
Worry less - free..the sunsets a sight.
Get to the yard and have a play around..
Shoot some hoops, roll on the ground.

The late nights of crickets chirping aloud
The mozzies buzzing past, owls hooting their
sounds.
The tapping from inside
Of mums spud mashing spoon
The call of 'dinners ready!'
And that grass itch that grew..
It was scoff down your dinner and get in the tub.
"Wash of that muck you feral little grub"
The water felt hot because your feet were now
cold.
But you needed a bath cos the grass itch took
hold.
"Stop scratching yourself and get in the water"
You'd sit down your bottom and felt like it had
scolded ya'

"Stop whinging it's hot" Mum would say.
"It's cos your body's cold - you've been outside
all day,
You didn't come in when I called you at 5-
It was cold by 6 and mozzies ate you alive.
The sun went down half 7

and it's now well past 8.
I called you in hours ago, your cold because
your late".

Before she could talk any more
my body had adjust,
The water was nearly cold actually.
The heat- Id soaked it up.

Get ready for bed then -
Plan adventures for the next day
Oh how I wish I could go back to those care-free
summer days.

www.ingramcontent.com/pod-product-compliance
Lightning Source LLC
Chambersburg PA
CBHW051743130826
49812CB00033B/980
* 9 7 8 9 3 9 5 9 5 0 1 2 1 *